A Family Life Nature Series

The Gospel According to a BLADE OF GRASS

By Terry & Jean McComb

Illustrations by Vera McMurdo

ISBN-13: 978-1-4796-1240-6 (Paperback)
ISBN-13: 978-1-4796-1241-3 ((ePub)
Library of Congress Control Number: 2023916633

Illustrations by Vera McMurdo

Published by

Table of Contents

Please Notice Carefully

The book in your hands is a multi-lesson teaching device that will involve the parent, grandparent, or teacher in a family-type activity in God's Outdoor Classroom.

Each page is a stand-alone lesson that is: 1) a reading lesson, 2) a character lesson, 3) a Bible lesson, 4) a science lesson, and 5) an art lesson (color the picture) per page.

Each lesson is created to have the parent/teacher take the child outside and share the lesson by the real object of nature under study. The lesson can be tailored either up or down, based on the child's level of experience and understanding. Later have them carefully color the art opposite the text. The Practical Project accomplished outside will awaken curiosity to desire to know the Creator Who made such a wonderful object of nature.

The art page may be photocopied for classroom use but not for resale.

This resource is excellent for Sunday/Sabbath school use or Boy/Girl Scout Club devotions. VBS leaders will find these lessons very useful. Also, pastors can use these in the children's story time in the worship service. Have the child color the picture while the pastor preaches, thus doubling the attention span of any child.

"God has shown His invisible attributes, His eternal power, and divine nature, clearly by what He has made. People are without an excuse for not glorifying God as Creator and giving Him gratitude and thanks" (Romans 1:20–21, McComb paraphrase).

ENJOY!!

Preface

In God's wonderworld of nature some miracles go unnoticed because they are so common. A blade of grass is such a wonder. A student of nature often learns only the name, identity, and anatomy of an object.

An area or nature study often missed is the way of an object. The ways have to do with its lifestyle and how it functions. It also includes how it interacts with the rest of God's wonderworld of nature.

In this book we shall look at some of the ways of grass and discover that they reveal some of the ways of its Maker. "You visit the earth and water it; You greatly enrich it; The river of God is full of water; You provide their grain, for so You have prepared it. You water its ridges abundantly, You settle its furrows; You make it soft with showers, You bless its growth. You crown the year with Your goodness, and Your paths drip with abundance. They drop on the pastures of the wilderness, and the little hills rejoice on every side. The pastures are clothed with flocks; the valleys also are covered with grain; they shout for joy, they also sing" (Psalm 65:9–13).

According to Holy Scriptures, grass was the first life He created in His new world. It appears to be the foundation for all that lives and breathes on planet Earth. This green, living machine quietly feeds and ministers to all; from the cows chewing their cud, all the way to the richest tycoon of Wall Street. All depend upon the humble grass for its contribution.

The authors encourage parents, teachers, and grandparents to enjoy this book with the child. Go with them into the out-of-doors classroom. Share these lessons with the child at the child's age level. Together, enjoy the character, science, Bible, and art lessons as each page unfolds. May this multi-learning experience cultivate seeing eyes and listening ears. May we hear the grasses "shout for joy", and in its rustling hear the message, "God is love."

Design

Many have left the rolling hills and the valleys of green to dwell in man-made cities of concrete and steel. The sweet aroma of fresh mown clover has been exchanged for the stench of burning exhaust. The warble of a meadowlark has been drowned out by the pulsating scream of a siren. From the freedom of the fields, our homes today are often on a cramped corner of lawn. Our original home made by God was a garden. It was very good. Even though we have departed from God's countryside to dwell in man-made cities, His love and wisdom can still be found right in a front lawn or a vacant lot.

A blade of grass is a marvelous example of architectural wonder. The height is often 500 times its diameter. If the Washington Monument were built in like proportions, its base would cover an area smaller than this book. Yet grass, a slip of green, towering into the heavens, uses not one guy wire for support. Blown down, stepped on, sat upon, yet it springs back. "He has made the earth by His power; He has established the world by His wisdom, and stretched out the heavens by His understanding" (Jeremiah 51:15).

Packed within this upright ribbon of green can be found some of nature's most elegant machinery. Powered by the sun, it purifies the air and helps feed our hungry world. If God can design, build and maintain this miniature tower by His wisdom, would we not be wise to follow His plans and His word in every area of our lives? We would be wise to let God have His way, not just with our lawns, but with our hearts.

PRACTICAL PROJECT

Go into the outdoor classroom and see if you can find grass that is 500 to 1 (500 times higher than its width). Look at its design carefully. This is something created by God! Observe and marvel.

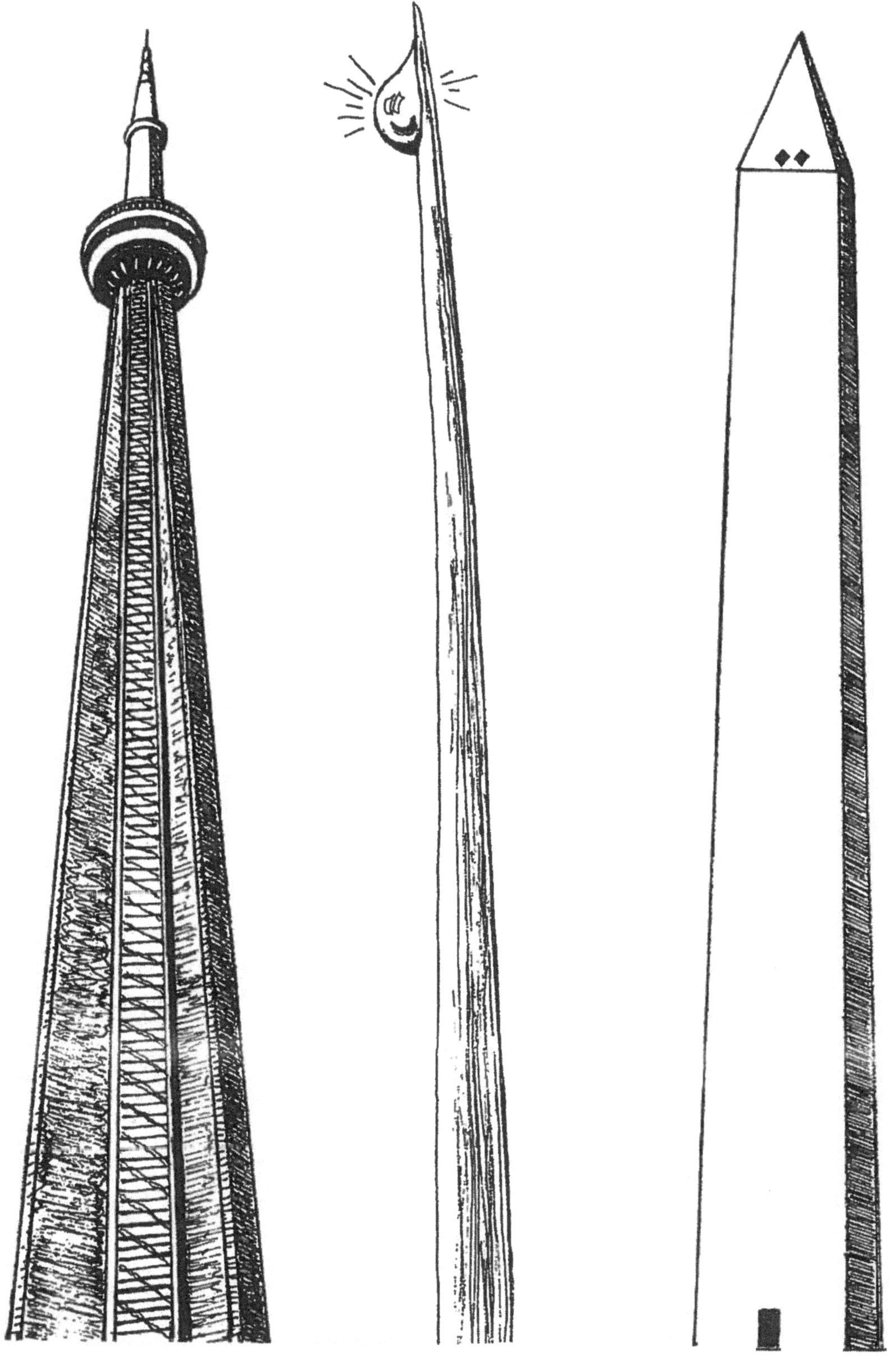

How Grass Originated

When our world was just three days old, God made grass. "Then God said, 'Let the earth bring forth grass, the herb that yields seed,' ...And the earth brought forth grass and herb that yields seed...So the evening and the morning were the third day" (Genesis 1:11–13).

A truth often lost, is that God created all things through His Son, Jesus Christ. Jesus was the One who spoke grass into existence. "For by Him all things were created that are in heaven and that are on earth, visible and invisible" (Colossians 1:16).

When the sun arose the third time, Jesus designed and created a blade of grass, along with the trees and other vegetation. With what cautious respect and awe should we consider the grass that Jesus thought was worth making. Its design, its purpose, its ways, should reveal some of the work and ways of Divinity.

The grass family's scientific name is Gramineae and consists of some 7,500 species. It is one of the largest families in the plant world.

What was the purpose for which God created grass and vegetation? It was to be food for man and animal. "And God said, 'See, I have given you every herb that yields seed which is on the face of all the earth, and every tree whose fruit yields seed: to you it shall be for food. Also, to every beast of the earth, to every bird of the air, and to everything that creeps on the earth, in which there is life, I have given every green herb for food'; and it was so" (Genesis 1:29, 30).

At creation the world was perfect. In a perfect world of no sin or death, all food for man and animal came from the plant kingdom. This was the original plan, fresh from the divine mind of Jesus.

PRACTICAL PROJECT

Go outside and pick a blade of grass to study. It was created by Jesus. Why its shape? Why its color? Note its texture. How well does it bend? What would our world look like without grass?

Purpose of Grass

All life on earth depends upon the living green. Grass grows without the aid of man, but Man cannot live without grass. Plants get their food from the soil, sun, and air. Grasses and other plants absorb approximately ten percent of the sun's energy. When animals, insects, rodents or man eat the plant, they receive only a fraction of the sun's energy that was stored there. Some creatures such as cows, sheep and some people get their food directly from the plants. Other creatures get their food by eating animals which have eaten plants. Cats and owls that eat mice would be in this group. Humans who eat meat would be in this second group also.

A third group are creatures of prey such as wild cats, wolves, and eagles. They eat the animals of the second group. God made garbage collectors for nature to take care of the dead. The hyena, vulture, pig, and raven are four of these scavengers.

Grass is the original food source. A rabbit eats grass. A weasel eats rabbits. A wild cat eats weasels. This process of one eating another is called a food chain.

About a dozen different grasses stock our supermarkets with cereal products, sugar, and snacks. They are made from the seeds of cereal grasses: rice, corn, oats, rye, wheat and barley. Sugar and molasses come from cane, which is also a grass. The big three grasses that feed the world are wheat, rice, and corn. Other foods also come indirectly from grasses by animals, such as meat or meant by-products, milk, cheese, and eggs. Non-edible products come from grasses by animals, such as leather goods, furs, and wool.

John James Ingalls, U.S. Senator from Kansas, put the urgency of grass this way. "Grass is the forgiveness of nature, her constant benediction...Should its harvest fail for a single year, famine would depopulate the world." We must have farmers who grow food from plants. One vital profession in our world is farming. We have twisted values. Farmers sell some of their products at World War II prices, yet at the same time we pay Hollywood stars millions to entertain us. We regularly raise the salaries of most professionals except farmers.

The Bible asks the question, "Why do you spend your money for that which is not bread?" (Isaiah 55:2). Farmers work with the original source of all foods; the plants. "He causes the grass to grow for the cattle, and vegetation for the service of man, that he may bring forth food from the earth" (Psalm 104:14).

PRACTICAL PROJECT

Keep a record of what your family eats for one day. How many different grasses did you eat? The food we eat does not grow in a grocery store. How much money does your family spend per week to buy grass products someone else grew?

CEREAL

Micro-organisms

Astonished, David Pramer of Rutgers University, looking through a powerful microscope, viewed a true drama. He focused in on a tiny, one-celled fungus plant and watched it lasso and strangle a ferocious Nema worm. The fungus plant had grown a thread 1/200 millimeter in thickness and strong as steel. The Nema came charging in and the plant formed a loop at the end of its thread and seized the dragon around the waist. The loop then inflated like a rubber innertube and strangled its victim. The fungus then dined leisurely on the carcass.

Invisible hordes of microscopic forms of life are waging constant war in the top soil of lawns and farmers' fields. Soil has the highest concentration of life on earth. An acre of typical farm soil six inches deep has: a ton of fungi, several tons of bacteria, 200 pounds of protozoa (one-celled animals), 100 pounds of algae and 100 pounds of yeast. The total mass of microbial life on earth is estimated to be 20 times greater than the total mass of animal life.

On a grain of lawn soil, these fantastic creatures live, battle, reproduce, and die. Each one is incredibly designed, having its special ministry to another form of life.

By eating dead plants and animals, they produce decay, which in turn releases locked up elements. These elements are used by plants. Therefore, a blade of grass lives and grows because of these unseen helpers. Plants then turn elements into vitamins and enzymes which are eaten by man and animals.

God uses these lowly unseen creatures and has made them vital to all known life. It is humbling for proud man to owe his very existence to the service of the God-made microscopic organisms.

They can live without us. We cannot live without them. "But God has chosen the foolish things of the world to put to shame the wise, and God has chosen the weak things of the world to put to shame the things which are mighty; and the base things of the world and the things which are despised God has chosen, and the things which are not, to bring to nothing the things that are, that no flesh should glory in His presence" (1 Corinthians 1:27–29).

PRACTICAL PROJECT

Go to your backyard and dig up a few tablespoons of topsoil. Spread it out onto some white paper. Look carefully with a picket magnifying glass. Do you see any sign of life? It teems with life largely unseen. Yet we owe our life to their ministry to the plant world.

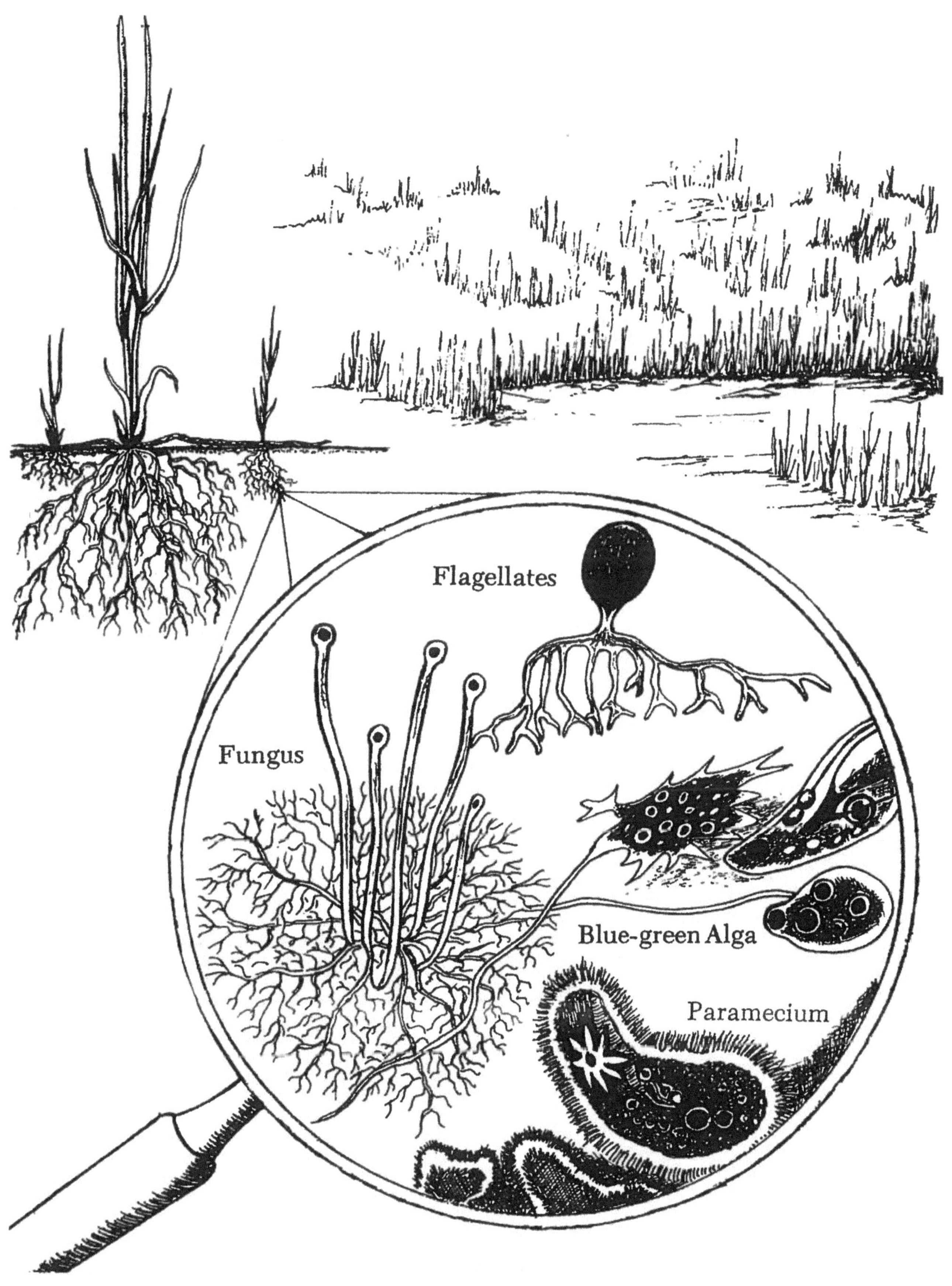
Flagellates
Fungus
Blue-green Alga
Paramecium

Green Link

God has ordained that grass and vegetation would be the connecting link between the mineral kingdom and the animal kingdom. Mineral substances can be changed into living tissues only by living organisms, such as grass, reaching down and taking the minerals up into themselves.

Man was made of the dust of the earth. "And the Lord God formed man of the dust of the ground, and breathed into his nostrils the breath of life; and man became a living being" (Genesis 2:7).

A human body of 154 pounds is composed of the following elements by weight:

Oxygen 97.20	Chlorine 0.25
Carbon 31.10	Fluorine 0.22
Hydrogen 15.20	Sulfur 0.22
Nitrogen 3.80	Potassium 0.18
Calcium 3.80	Magnesium 0.11
Phosphorus 1.75	Iron 0.01
And Other Trace Minerals	

While we are made up of mineral matter, we cannot sit down and eat mud pies or a dish of steaming dirt. Yet grasses take these elements and with the energy of the sun, and wisdom from above, change mud into wheat and dust into corn.

The first man and woman were originally created in the image of God. "So God created man in His own image; in the image of God He created him; male and female He created them" (Genesis 1:27).

When man sinned, he exchanged a loving relationship for a selfish one. He lost the ability to love like God. In order to restore the image of God back into man Jesus became human (see Philippians 2:5–8).

As grass is the connecting link between the mineral and the animal, Jesus is the connecting link between heaven and earth. No man can make himself divine or righteous. Jesus is the only mediator between God and man. "For there is one God and one Mediator between God and man, the Man Christ Jesus" (1 Timothy 2:5). So Jesus is the living link between heaven and earth. He takes that which is divine and holy and brings it down to this earth so humans can be saved by it.

How vainly they seek for His glory,
In creeds musty with age!
Why not welcome His story,
On nature's simple page?
I worship the God of the grasses,
Jesus both human and Divine,
My ignorance I link with His wisdom,
His forgiveness I find is mine.
Anonymous

PRACTICAL PROJECT

Plant a few radish seeds in some dirt placed in a paper cup. Water it (just nicely damp). Place in a window that receives sun light. Watch these tiny seeds change the inorganic soil into organic food in two weeks. How does it know how to do this? Prayer connects the human to the divine. Ponder!

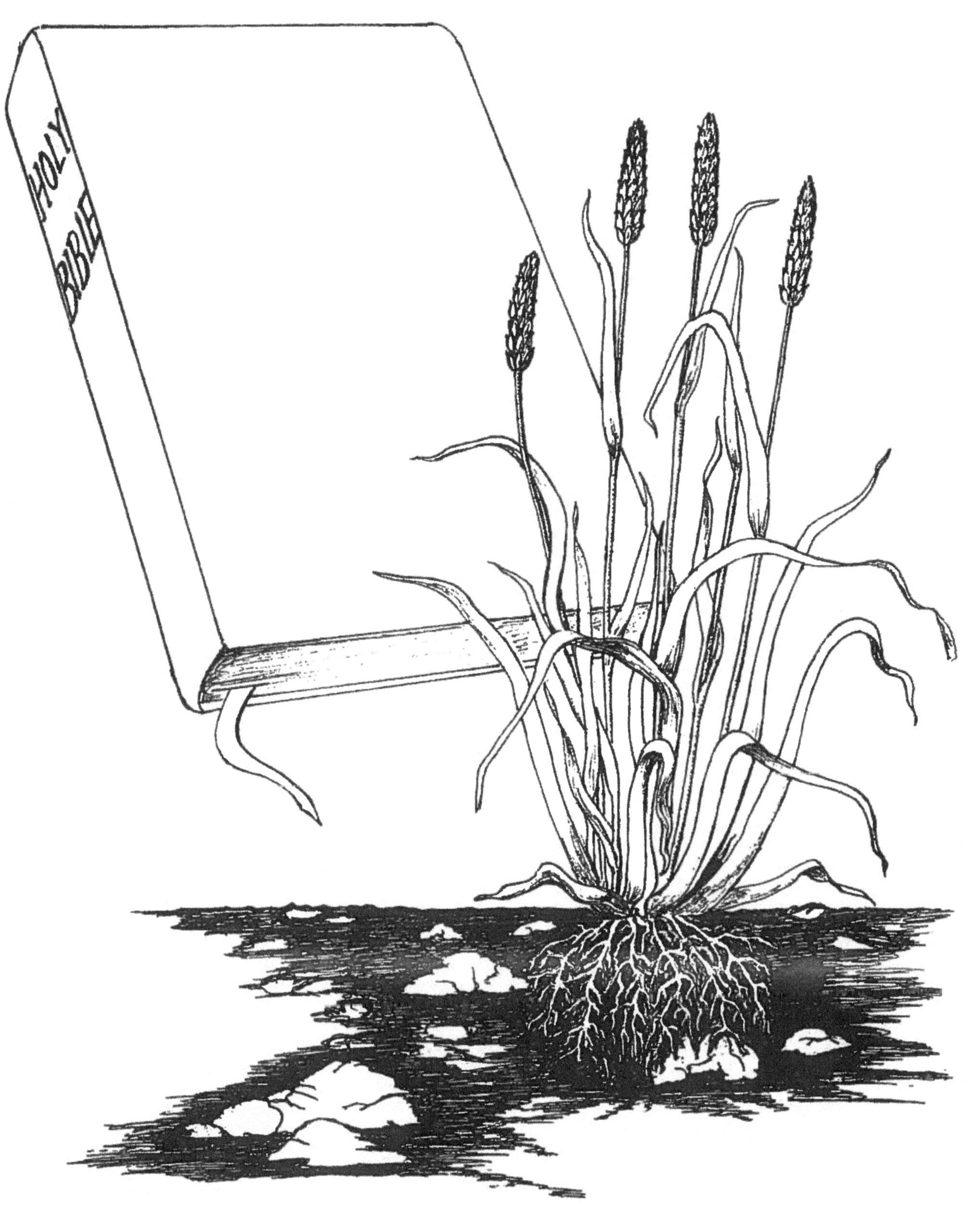
HOLY
BIBLE

Identifying Grass

On the opposite page are nine common grasses. You will see each are similar with long slender blades.

You will notice they are also very different. In the magnifying glass is shown the flower part of each grass. Each grass is special and this difference shows up best on the flower parts.

Each different member of the grass family has been given a name. The name given often describes some special characteristic of the plant. Each member of the grass family is made by God to be special and grows in a unique place or climate. Each has a unique work assigned to it by the Creator for the animal kingdom. Try and see if you can locate any of the nine grasses flowering near your home.

In a similar way, each child in your family is special. God makes each classmate at school different. Each one has talents, abilities, and capabilities for service to God and man.

Each child has been given a name by his parents. In Bible times parents gave their children a name to represent the character that they wanted their child to have. Try looking up the meaning of your name. Then attach a Biblical character meaning to your name.

My name is Terry. Its cultural meaning is "smooth polish one." My Biblical character meaning would be "one being polished." A Bible text that would go with my character meaning could be "When He has tested me, I shall come forth as gold" (Job 23:10). If you have a Bible concordance try finding a passage that fits the meaning of your name.

As God has created and named every grass of the field so He has made each one of us. He knows us by our name. "Thus says the Lord who created you...Fear not, for I have redeemed you. I have called you by your name: You are Mine" (Isaiah 43:1).

PRACTICAL PROJECT

See how many different kinds of grass grow in your lawn, around the house, or at school. Do the "Name project" and find the character meaning of your name. Make a plaque with your character name, a Bible text, and hang on your bedroom wall.

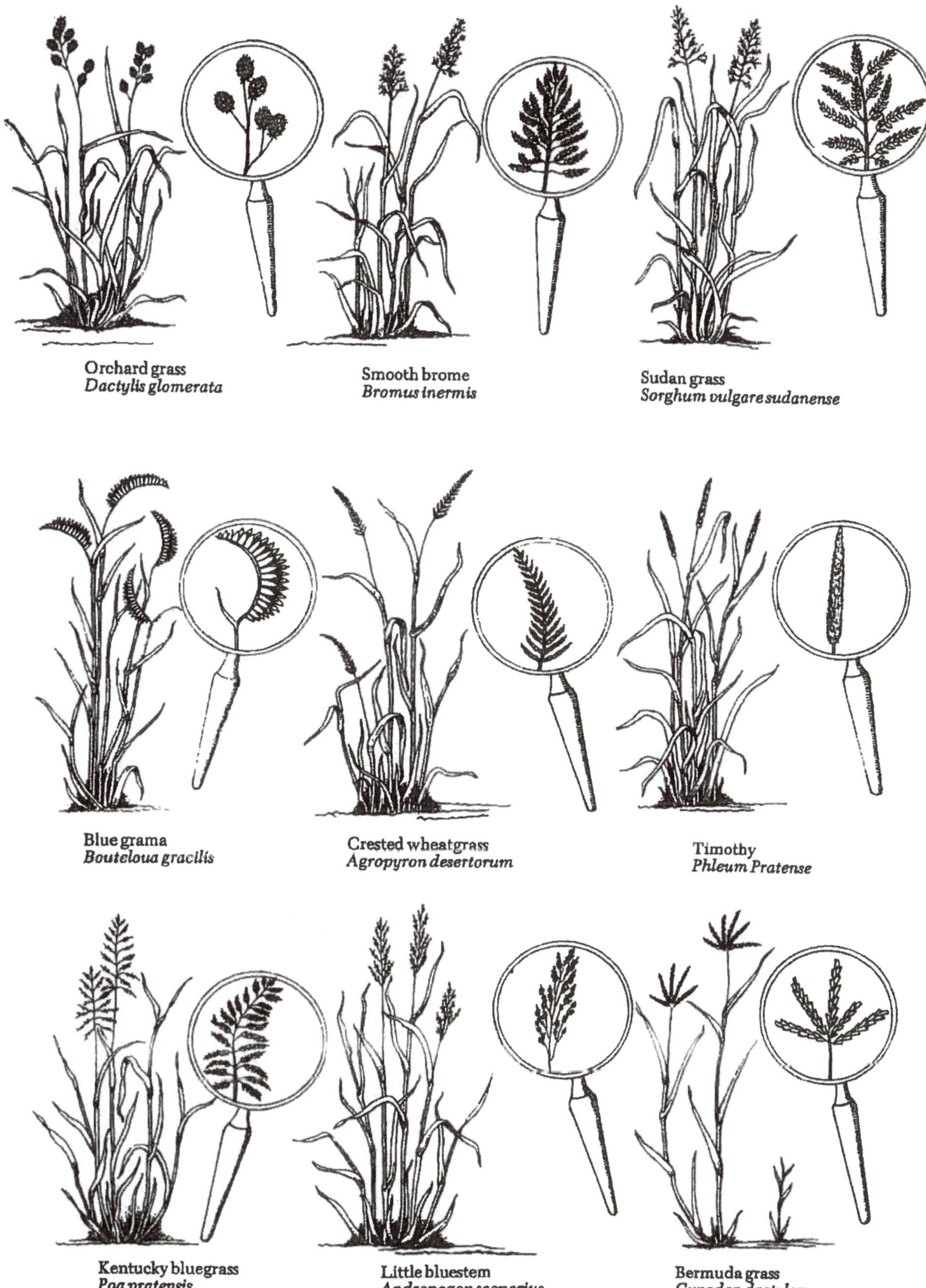
Orchard grass
Dactylis glomerata
Smooth brome
Bromus inermis
Sudan grass
Sorghum vulgare sudanense
Blue grama
Bouteloua gracilis
Crested wheatgrass
Agropyron desertorum
Timothy
Phleum Pratense
Kentucky bluegrass
Poa pratensis
Little bluestem
Andropogon scoparius
Bermuda grass
Cynodon dactylon

Anatomy of Grass

The roots of grasses are used to hold the plant to the soil, and the soil to the plant, holding it upright as it is swayed to and fro by the wind. And from the soil the roots soak up minerals, nutrients, and water like a sponge. At the same time, they give back to the soil enriching nutrients. This maintains the plant's life and, as the roots grow, they may also reproduce new plants.

The stem and blade are the tower part of the plant. The blade collects the sun's rays and gives off oxygen for humans and animals to breathe.

The flower part produces seeds. The goal of the plant, is the perpetuation of the species. Sow a seed of grass such as wheat and it may produce 100 times itself or more. This super-natural multiplication is what feeds the animal kingdom on this earth.

The different parts of this living spire all function together in service to God and man. They provide food and air for God's creatures and, in this way, grass brings glory to God its Maker and happiness to man and animal. Grass provides this same service whether growing on the land of a king, or in a ditch at the city dump.

Man, likewise has an anatomy. But his anatomy of head, body, arms and legs are much different from grass even though they function together and were designed by the same Master designer.

As grass parts work together for service so our body parts are to function in service. This service may be by helping a stray kitten find a home or helping mother clean the house. The end result of our service should produce the fruit of joy.

However, teasing someone may bring joy to you; but may make someone else cry. The fruit that God is looking for is joy both to the doer and to the receiver. Both are to be happy.

If you will limit your freedom within the loving limits of God's holy law both of you will have full joy. The commandments tell how we are to serve God and how we are to serve others.

Christ's love in your heart will enable you to experience His joy. "By this is my Father glorified that you bear much fruit; so you will be My disciples. As the Father loved Me, I also have loved you; abide in My love, just as I have kept My Father's commandments and abide in His love. These things I have spoken to you, that my joy may remain in you, and that your joy may be full" (John 15:8–11).

PRACTICAL PROJECT

Pull up some grass and identify its parts using the picture on the opposite page.

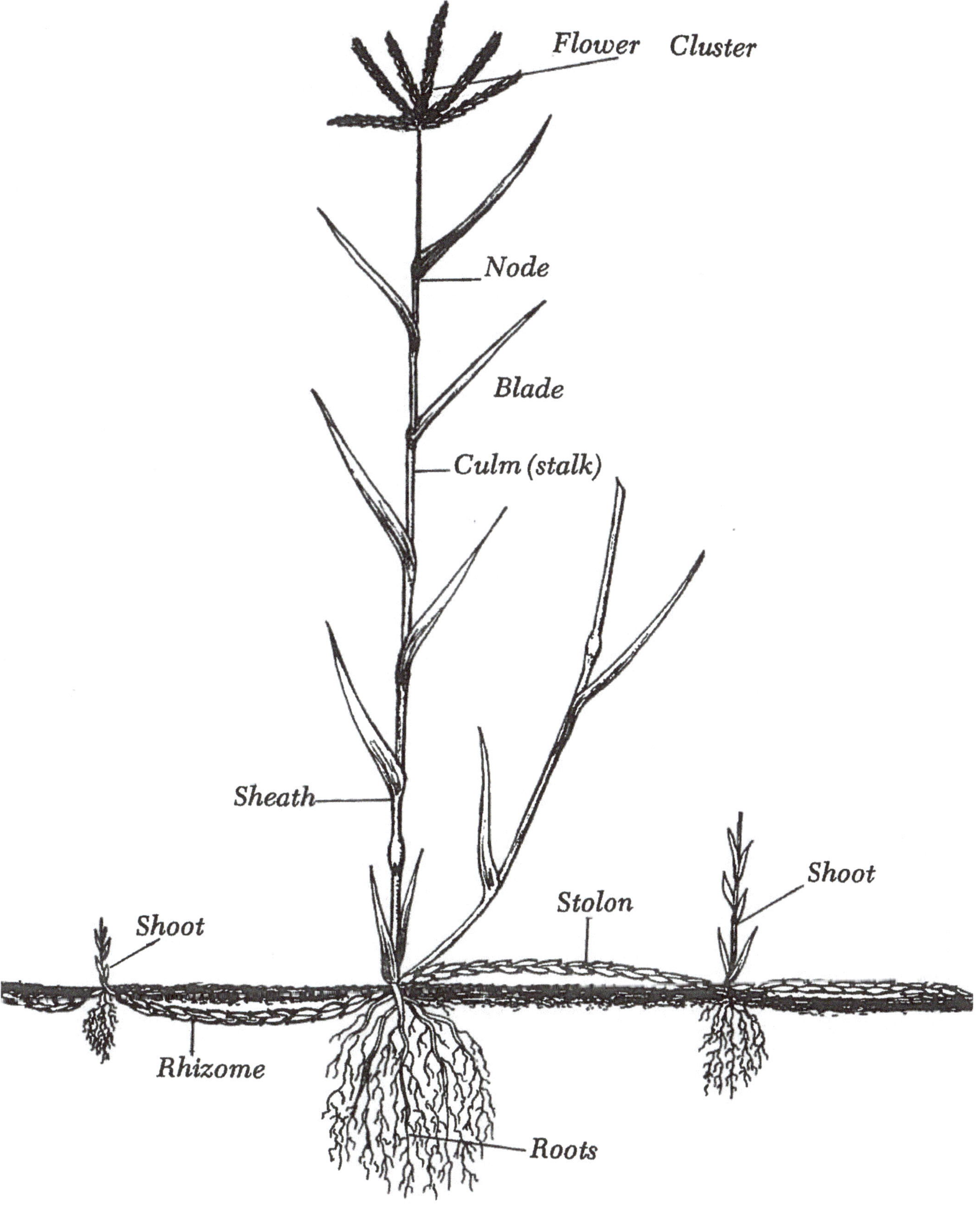
Flower Cluster
Node
Blade
Culm (stalk)
Sheath
Shoot
Stolon
Shoot
Rhizome
Roots

Closer Look

Grass at 50-power magnification reveals very careful engineering. God designed, created, and continues to build every blade of grass with as much care and perfection as when He created our galaxy.

One edge of grass may be saw-toothed. Each little point is perfect along its length. "Therefore you shall be perfect, just as your Father in heaven is perfect" (Matthew 5:48).

Using magnification, we look toward the middle of a blade of grass. Here we discover tiny hairs, each one just the right height, carefully placed on the vertical veins of the grass. All grasses have vertical veins. Tree leaves and other plants may have horizontal veins. These were created with great care and perfection. God never skimps on details, even for a blade of grass.

It is sometimes difficult for us to pay attention to the small matters of life while the mind is engaged in work of vast importance. This is not so with God. We can follow our Creator's example in giving the same care for little things as we do the big. "He who is faithful in what is least is faithful also in much; and he who is unjust in what is least is unjust also in much" (Luke 16:10).

Courtesy is a little thing that requires much care. We may become so busy as to neglect talk time with mom and dad. Parents may often feel too busy to listen. Talk time is where every member of the family stops what he is doing and sits down for a sharing time. One may listen while another reads a story. Children may like to tell what happened at school. Problems may be shared. By trial and error this carefully set-aside time may become a precious heritage.

PRACTICAL PROJECT

Use a high-power pocket magnifying glass or microscope and examine a blade of grass closely. (Surplus microscopes may be purchased from college or high school labs inexpensively.) Do you see evidence of careful design? As a family, turn off the TV and other diversions and spend 15 minutes just talking and listening. Care enough to share life—together!

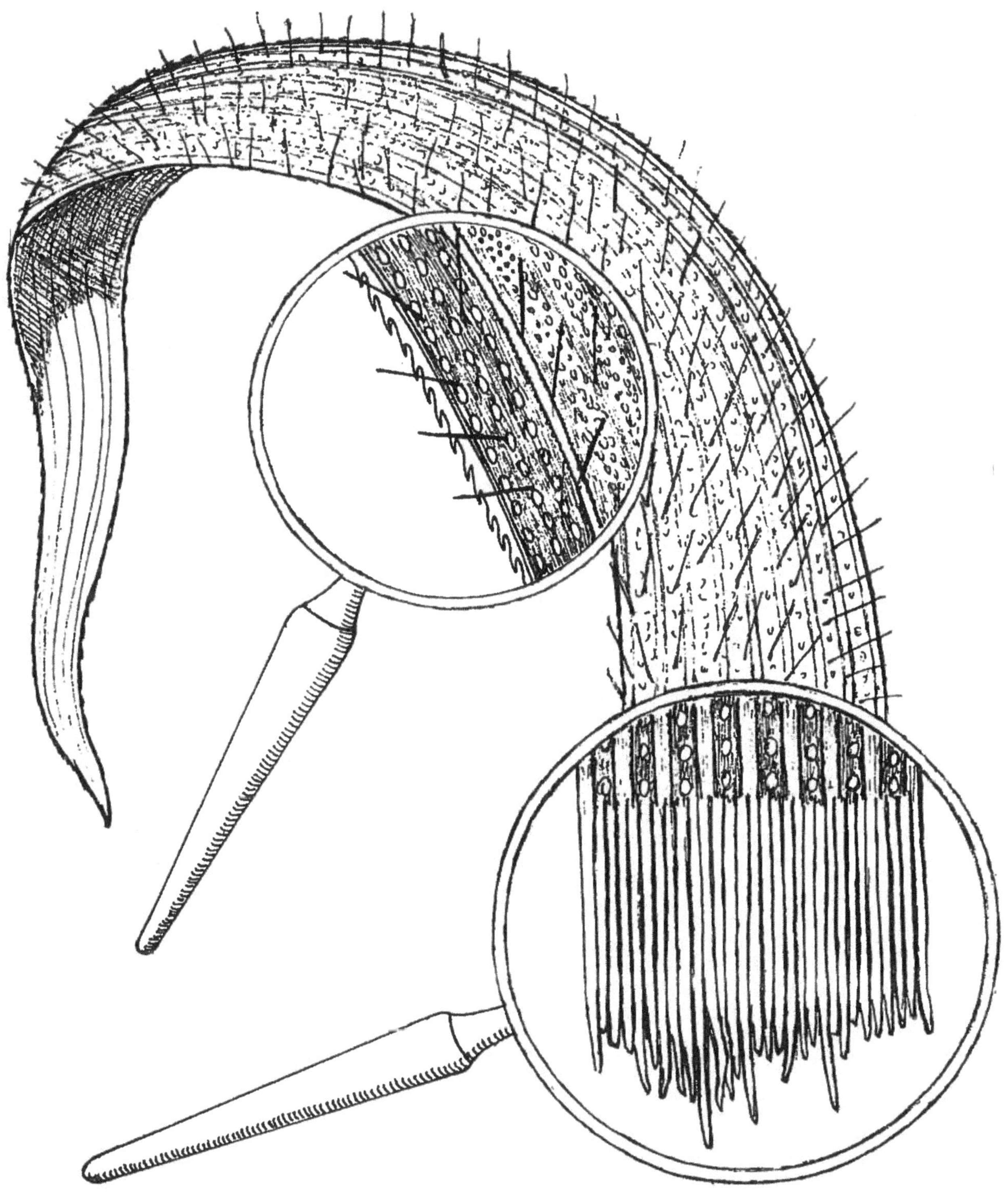

Photosynthesis

Under high magnification, little green circles or discs are seen from the bottom to the top of a blade of grass. These round discs are chloroplasts. Chloroplasts take in carbon dioxide and give off oxygen. This process is called photosynthesis. This word comes from two words—photo, meaning light, and synthesis meaning process. This process works as follows: the blade of grass takes in carbon dioxide on one side. Inside, the chloroplasts use energy from the sun to take the carbon out of the carbon dioxide. This carbon is stored in the leaves and seeds as energy called carbohydrates. These may be eaten in a fresh garden salad or in bread and other seeds. All life on earth is dependent on the silent work of these little chloroplasts. This purification system functions day after day taking in carbon dioxide, purifying it, and returning it back to us as oxygen.

Dr. Leonard Hard, Professor of biology at Andrews University, tells us that the by-product of photosynthesis is able to completely replace the oxygen in the atmosphere in our world once every two thousand years.

Jesus does a spiritual work for us similar to that of the chloroplasts. Jesus has enclosed our world with an atmosphere of grace that is as real as the air we breathe. The Holy Spirit is the medium of that grace which gives us the desire and power to do God's will.

Through prayer we may give our sins to Jesus by confession. "If we confess our sins, He is faithful and just to forgive us our sins and to cleanse us from all unrighteousness" (1 John 1:9). We give Him our sins and wrong desires and in exchange He gives us His forgiveness and a love without any tint of selfishness. "Do not be overcome by evil, but overcome evil with good" (Romans 12:21).

What a trade! This divine-human exchange is called salvation. "Let us therefore come boldly to the throne of grace, that we may obtain mercy and find grace to help in time of need" (Hebrews 4:16).

PRACTICAL PROJECT

If you can get access to a microscope, pick a fresh blade of grass and look at it in the sun light. At about 50 power magnification these bits of green will glow in living color! It takes some kind of living life to make this exchange. As a family, by living faith, lay hold of the power of the living Christ. Claim His unfailing promises as yours in family worship prayer. By the Holy Spirit, His love will become the life of your family.

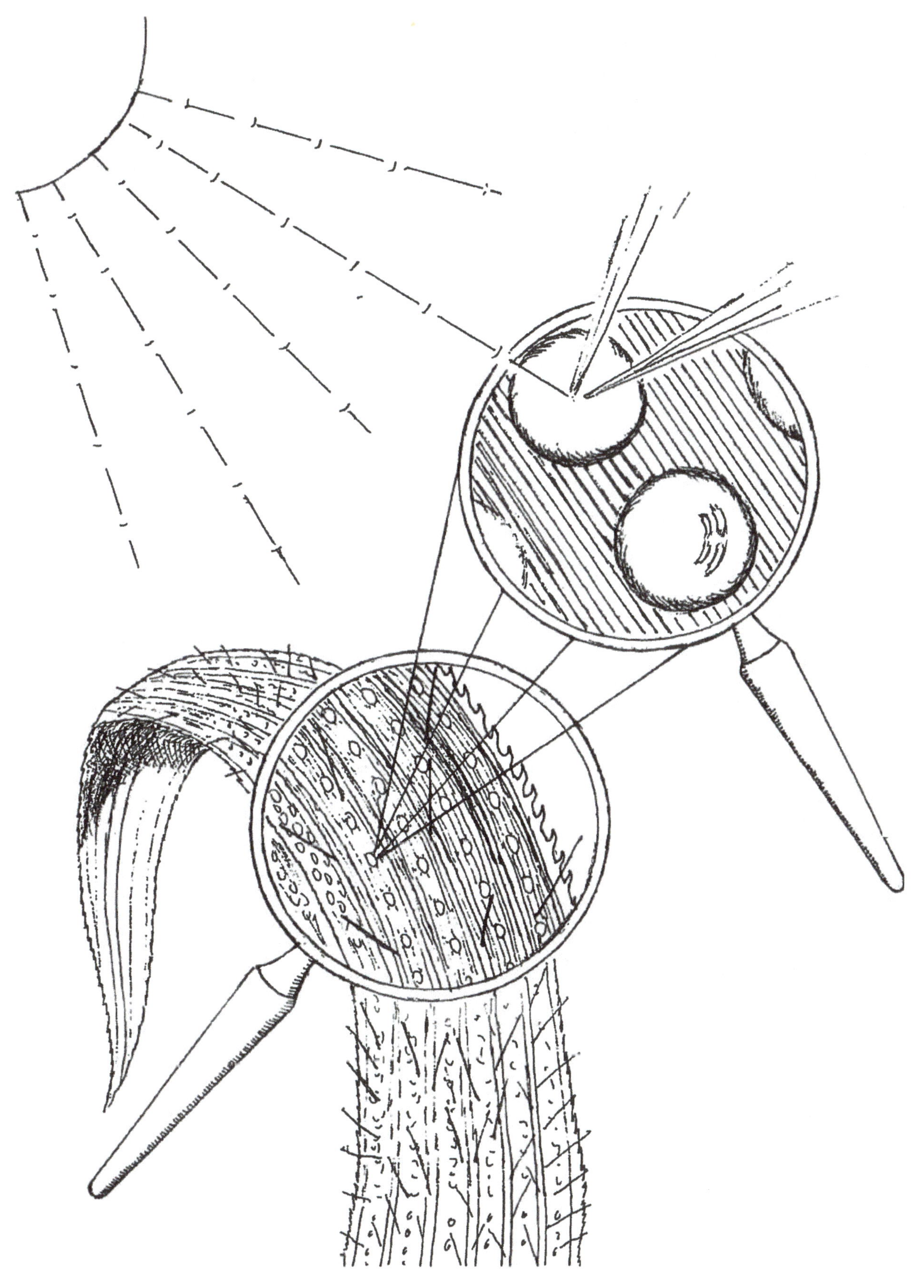

Stoma of Grass

To the lover of suspense and mystery, no field is more open to investigation than the field of nature. Under the scrutiny of an electron microscope, a blade of grass reveals many mysteries.

On the top of the blade we see little openings. In the book, *Being a Plant*, by Lawrence Pringle, we are told that a blade of grass may have 8,000 little openings per centimeter. These little openings are stomata, which means little mouths. Stomata vary from plant to plant. A corn or cucumber leaf may have about twice as many as grass.

Leaves that grow in the shade have fewer stomata than those do in bright sunlight. These openings allow the water vapor and gases to come and go through the leaf of the plant.

It has been estimated that an acre of grass can give off as much as six tons of water a day. On a rainy day it may absorb almost the same amount of water.

A blade of grass may add or take out water from the air. At the same time, it can cool the air like an air conditioner. This air conditioner operates on solar power without care or concern of busy man.

Much of how the stomata operate still remains a mystery. Scientists admit that there are many unknowns in a blade of grass.

In a similar way, there are many mysteries in the Bible. The Bible is a book about the Creator of all science. If we have a hard time understanding grass, certainly, we will have a hard time understanding the Author Himself.

"And without controversy great is the mystery of godliness" (1 Timothy 3:16). Jesus came to do for us spiritually what the electron microscope does for us physically. He came to make clearer God's love.

PRACTICAL PROJECT

Try to get access to a higher power microscope to see these stomata. Don't take the awe away from our Creator. It is wisdom to humbly say "I don't know."

Electron micrograph by Harold Clark

Grass Flowers

Lawn grass has flowers. We rarely see them because grass is mowed before the flower stage is reached. The opposite picture shows the flower and seed of a type of grass called foxtail. The flower parts of grass are what produce its seed.

Most grass flowers open in the morning. The stamen opens quickly during this time, sometimes growing twice its length in ten minutes.

Wheat has flowers that open only once in a lifetime and then only for fifteen minutes. All the wheat flowers in a field must open at this same period of time in order to be cross-pollinated.

Our life also is a once-in-a-lifetime opportunity to accept Christ. No second lives are offered. "It is appointed for men to die once, but after this the judgment" (Hebrews 9:27).

Our time of life is lived one moment at a time. Not one moment can be relived. Time is a form of grace we don't earn or deserve. All receive and spend the same amount daily from Adam until now.

Seeds, like time, have potential. A kernel of wheat is not a wheat plant or a harvest. It is potentially a plant or harvest. Time is like seeds; what we do with our moments determines what we will reap in life. If you waste two hours each evening for 75 years you will have wasted 54,750 hours of your time. That amount of time would earn the equivalent of 20 college degrees.

Remember the flower on a head of wheat the next time you butter your toast. The once-in-a-lifetime flowering happening at exactly the right moment reminds us of the seriousness of sowing good seeds. "Do not be deceived, God is not mocked; whatsoever a man sows, that he will also reap. For he who sows to his flesh will of the flesh reap corruption, but he who sows to the Spirit will of the Spirit reap everlasting life. And let us not grow weary while doing good, for in due season we shall reap if we do not lose heart" (Galatians 6:9).

PRACTICAL PROJECT

As a family, choose to earn a college degree by using one hour per evening to become authorities in some field of nature. Turn off the TV and DVDs. Enjoy learning together.

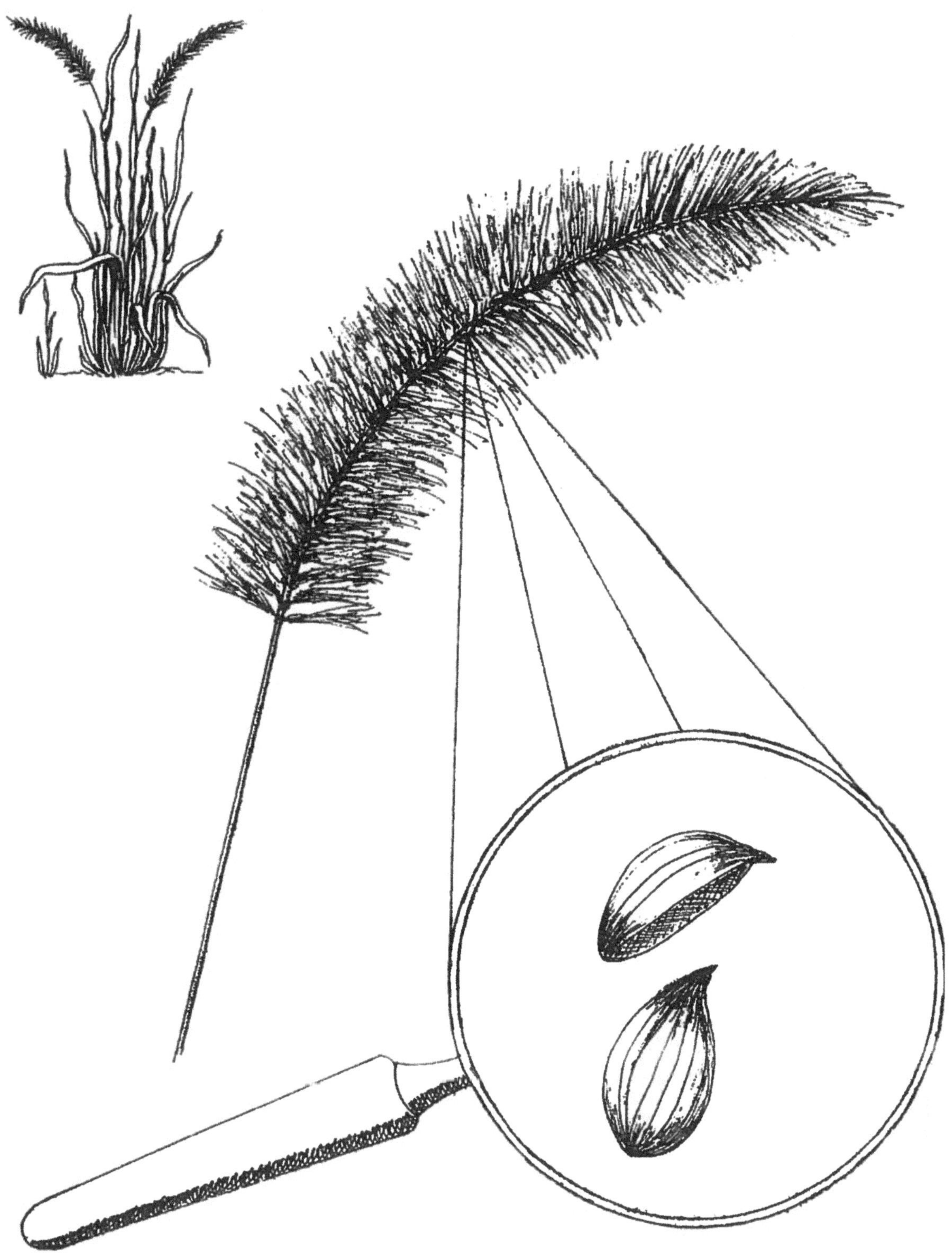

New Growth

By His Word, God created grass as He created this earth. By this Word He gives it power to grow and multiply. That Word still causes the seed to grow. Every seed that sends up its green blade to the sunlight declares the wonderworking power of that Word. "For He spoke, and it was done; He commanded, and it stood fast" (Psalm 33:9).

Have you ever passed a field of corn and noticed a tiny blade pushing its way to the surface in spite of heavy clods of earth? Have you seen the baked earth heave up? Under it was a tiny spire. This spire was so tender it could not support its own weight. This blade was but little more than water. If you had crushed it in your fingers, there would have been scarcely anything left but moisture on your hand. Yet this tiny thing was pushing away a clod of earth ten thousand times its own weight.

Where does this power come from? Is there something inherent in the grass? Try this and see.

Take a blade of grass that is full-grown. Select a small clod of dirt and put it on top of the grass. What happens? The grass is crushed to the ground. It was no power in itself. Try it again. Take that tiny blade and put it on your hand and it will lop over the side. It cannot even stand upright, yet a few moments before it was standing erect bearing a burden many times heavier than itself. This miracle is wrought millions of times every year.

It is in obedience to the law of God that the spire of grain bursts through the ground, "first the blade, then the head, after that the full grain in the head." These the Lord develops in their proper season.

PRACTICAL PROJECT

Do the above. Take a clear plastic cup and plant some beans that have soaked for 24 hours. Watch the sprout push its way through the soil in the cup. Place a penny on top. How many coins will it take to stop growth?

New and Old Grass

The relationship between a blade of grass and its roots is an illustration of how God would have our relationship be with our extended family.

For sake of illustration, observe how roots function in a role similar to grandparents. Blades of grass perform a role similar to parents; new shoots of grass grow in a way like children.

Grass roots live about 20 years. At death, they decompose and their lifetime collection of fibers and nutrients are returned to the soil. Approximately one-third of these roots will die annually, thus enriching the soil with an estimated ten tons of dry weight organic fertilizer per acre.

In a similar way, grandparents pass on to their children their lifetime collection of valuables. Usually, this is thought of in terms of house, land, and money. However, the most valuable gift they can give to their children and to their children's children is their lifetime collection of values and godly wisdom.

A mother and grandmother recorded their favorite stories. Their grandchildren, thousands of miles away, listen to these stories. These grandchildren listen to these stories over and over again. In Deuteronomy 6:2, 7, God commanded grandparents to teach their children and grandchildren His ways.

The last great reformation (see Isaiah 58:12) will restore the breach between God's ways and man's ways by parents teaching their children and their grandchildren the ways of the Creator. His values and truths are a safe foundation upon which to build young lives. They are eternal.

Young grass shoots grow rapidly on the accumulated fertilizer provided by past generations of grass. In a similar way, wise will be the youth that will build his young life-style upon his forefather's foundation of godly ways. "Honor your father and your mother, that your days may be long upon the land which the Lord your God is giving you" (Exodus 20:12).

PRACTICAL PROJECT

Ask your Grandparents to share their wisdom of Scripture and life by letter, a recording, or a visit. Ask them to make a scrapbook of their married wisdom.

Root System

More than one-third of the grass plant grows underground in the form of roots. These form a stable foundation for the plant to grow on.

Botanists grew winter rye in a box containing two cubic feet of soil. In four months, the slender grass grew 20 inches tall. During this same time the main roots, if laid end to end, would reach a length of 373 miles. The root hairs would be 6,000 miles long. The combined absorbing area was estimated at nearly twice the size of a tennis court.

With such long fingers, the roots firmly anchor the plant to the soil and the soil to the plant. Neither can easily be blown or washed away by wind or rain. Some grass roots grow more than ten feet long. With this extensive underground system, the plant absorbs nutrients and moisture from the soil.

The Christian, likewise, is to be "rooted and built up in Him [Christ]" (Colossians 2:7). We are to be "rooted and grounded in Christ's love" (Ephesians 3:17).

Strength for victory over sin comes from above. A divine power outside of ourselves is to come in and transform us. We are to grow more dependent daily upon the agencies of the Holy Bible, the Holy Spirit and the ministry of the holy angels. These will work like the roots of the grass to fasten us to Jesus. The more we exercise our minds to think on scripture, the more we become rooted in His love.

As the roots of grass absorb nutrients so we are to allow the Holy Spirit to penetrate every area of our lives.

Roots are a major way lawn grass reproduces itself. Likewise, the Christian is commanded to go make disciples of all men (see Matthew 28:19, 20). When we are rooted and grounded in Christ we will have something to tell of what Jesus has done for us.

If the root grows above the ground and starts another plant it is called a stolon. If the root grows underground and starts a new plant it is called a rhizome. In a similar way, the Christian who goes to another country to share what Christ has done for him is called a missionary. However, if we live like Jesus at home and school, we shall be called a friend and neighbor.

PRACTICAL PROJECT

As a family, choose someone to be your mission field, someone that needs to be loved for Christ. The family next door? Across the street? Across town? How can you share Jesus with them?

Mown Grass

Freshly mown grass gives off a delightful spicy fragrance. A fresh cut field of hay smells of sweet odors. Mowing a lawn can stimulate growth. This is because a blade of grass grows from the bottom not the top. When the top of the spire is cut, it builds a new blade at its base, thus pushing the whole structure upward. By the way, engineers would delight to build a skyscraper with that kind of technology.

Similar to grass, as Christians, we are to grow from the inside out. We are to accept Christ's principles first in our minds and, later, these qualities will show on the outside, by our words and actions. When cut or hurt by unkind words we may emit the fragrance of a soft answer that turns away wrath. When we suffer a sudden loss or tragedy, faith is an aroma that we can manifest.

At times we may feel like a blade of grass that has been cut. Our best friend may move away or may say cutting unkind things to us. This loss can be sweetened by counting it a joy. "My brethren, count it all joy when you fall into various trials, knowing that the testing of your faith produces patience. But let patience have its perfect work, that you may be perfect and complete, lacking nothing" (James 1:2–4).

When grass is cut, nature at once begins to repair the injury. Before this loss, God-given healing agencies were ready. Likewise, before sin came, heaven had a plan of salvation ready. Christ's mission to this world was one of healing (see Luke 4:18). Someone in our family can be hurt physically, mentally, or spiritually. We may become one of Christ's healing agencies. By our kindness and sympathy, we can help them bear their pain or loss.

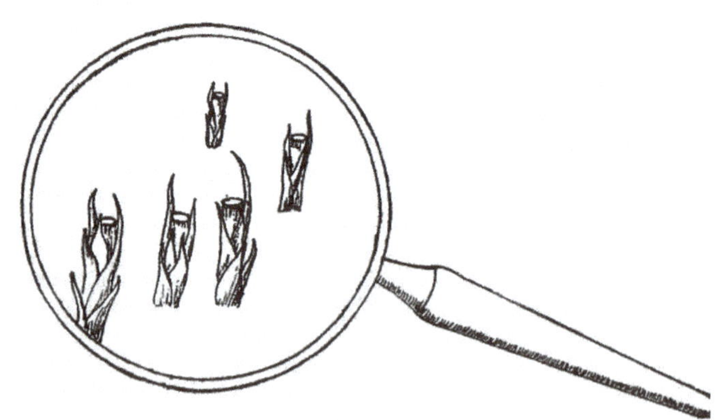

 PRACTICAL PROJECT

Pick some grass and crush it in your hand, then smell. Try different kinds of grass or leaves. Do they all smell the same? Try a rose flower crushed up, then smell. Jesus, when abused, revealed His Father's love. As a family, let us overcome evil with His goodness.

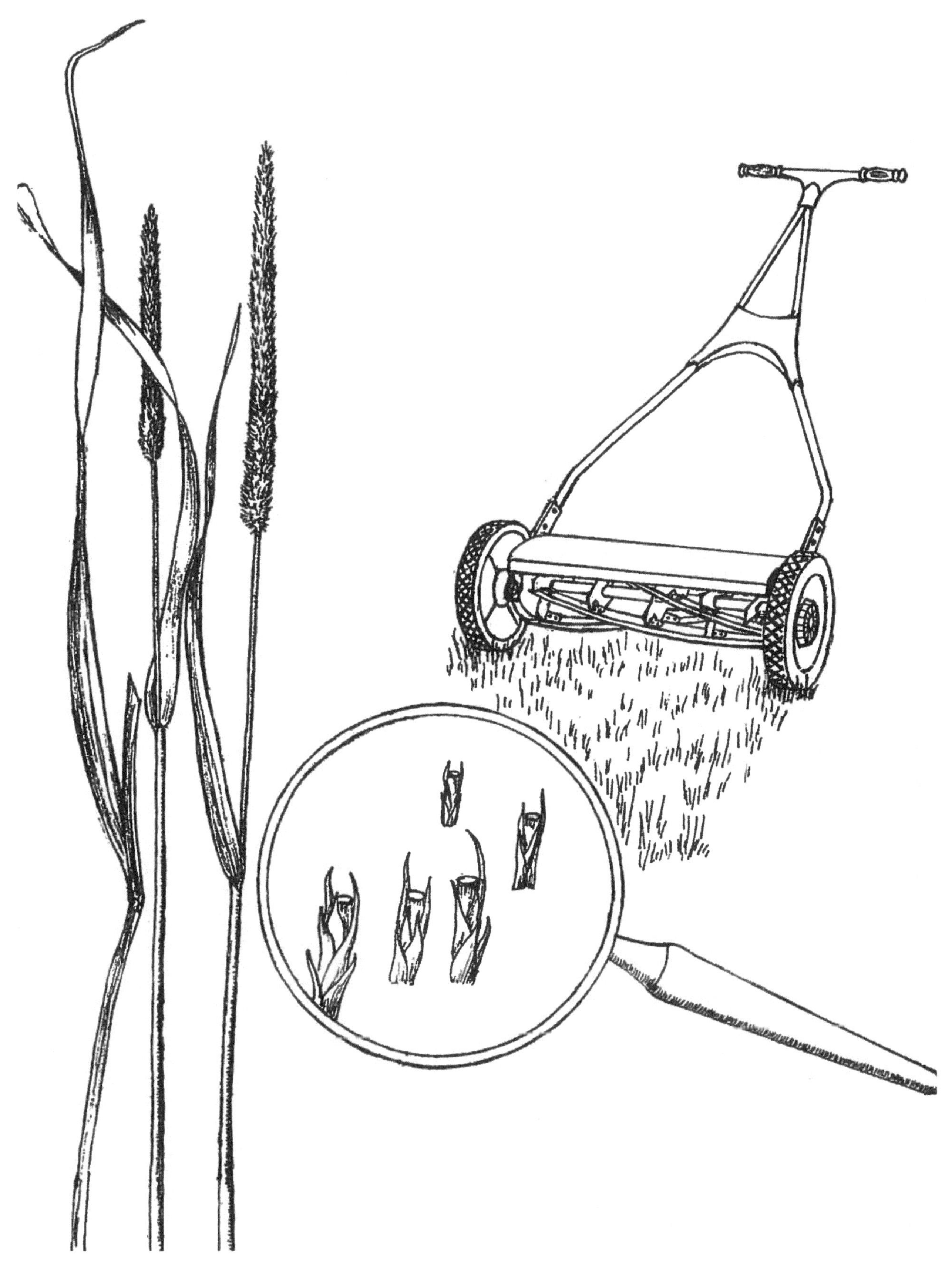

Beauty of Dry Grass

Grass is often used in scripture to illustrate the shortness of life. "All flesh is grass, and all its loveliness is like the flower of the field. The grass withers, the flower fades... Surely the people are grass. But the word of our God stands forever" (Isaiah 40:6–8).

Men erect memorials to honor those who have done great things. Grass likewise leaves a memorial of beautiful brown leaves after it dies. These died grasses can be collected together to make beautiful floral displays. Some of these grasses are almost as pretty when dead as when they were alive. The cellulose structure that remains tells us something of the beauty that once graced the living plant.

Panic grass has tiny black seeds. They remain on the brown stems and leaves after the plant dies. These seeds will become a living memorial to how the plant lived. Seeds will produce another plant like the parent.

In a similar way, children become living memorials to their parents. The parents may grow old and die, but the descendants live on. "Blessed are the dead who die in the Lord from now on. "Yes," says the Spirit, "that they may rest from their labors, and their works follow them" (Revelation 14:13).

Wealthy people cannot take their money with them when they die. Everything they have is left behind for others to use. "For no sooner has the sun risen with a burning heat than it withers the grass; its flower falls, and its beautiful appearance perishes. So the rich man also will fade away in his pursuits" (James 1:11).

Grass dies out in the fall like a symbol of death. At springtime, fresh green grass will replace the brown stubble representing a memorial of hope in the resurrection. How a fresh green shoot can spring forth out of apparent dead roots seems a mystery. This yearly miracle is certain, and so is the resurrection. "Behold, I tell you a mystery: We shall not all sleep, but we shall all be changed in a moment, in the twinkling of an eye, at the last trumpet. For the trumpet will sound, and the dead will be raised incorruptible, and we shall be changed" (1 Corinthians 15:51).

PRACTICAL PROJECT

Collect dried grasses and try making floral arrangements for your table. Try to arrange them with glue to make a picture to frame for the wall. As a family, visit a graveyard and read the epitaphs on the tombstones. What do we want said on our stone?

A Grass-side Society

Grass in the countryside is a home for many creatures. It is estimated that the population on an acre of North American prairie in midsummer is around ten million insects. Where insects are, the birds follow. The killdeer is a bird of the grasslands. It builds its nest right among the grasses. Grass gives protection to insects, birds, rodents, and snakes. Each one living in this grass society ministers to the life of another.

God has made their grass home beautiful. He could have made grass red, pink, or black. Instead, it is a beautiful green, the color most restful to the eye. This elegant spire becomes even lovelier when it sways in the wind.

God has clothed the structure of this earth with soil, and then He covered the brown and black soil with lush living green.

For an interesting project, take a space of lawn about the size of this book and observe how many things grow there. In a few moments, I observed more than ten tiny cobwebs strung between blades of grass. They gave off the iridescent colors of the rainbow. I found a dozen other things. A wounded fly came by, two golden ants, and the seed of a cattail were found. I saw the eggs of many different types of bugs and insects on the blades of grass. Grass is a host to a whole community of living creatures.

Could you imagine trying to prepare enough food at your house to feed ten million guests?

If God provides the grass-side society with this lovely house of green, will He not also take care of you and me? "Now if God so clothes the grass of the field, which today is, and tomorrow is thrown into the oven, will He not much more clothe you, O you of little faith?" (Matthew 6:30).

PRACTICAL PROJECT

Let each member of the family choose a one-foot square piece of green lawn to study. Who can find the most different kinds of life in your one-foot space? Try the same on different kinds of lawns. Do some have more life than others?

Dew and Guttation

Have your feet ever gotten wet on a chilly morning walk? You may have thought that the grass was covered with dew. Actually, this wetness may not have been dew at all, but guttation. At times grass will have a droplet of water right on the very tip of the blade. If the night is humid and cool, the vapor could not become part of the air as rapidly as it came out of the leaf, so it collects right at the end of the blade of grass as a droplet. The rest of the blade will have no water at all. Dew, on the other hand, makes water droplets all over the blade of grass. Guttation is when water vapor comes out of the plant rather than out of the air.

Often, people think dew falls from the sky during the night because it is seen only in the morning. Dew does not fall out of the sky, but from the air around us. In dew, water vapor condenses on cool grass, becoming droplets all over the blade. Dew and guttation illustrate a principle of Christianity.

There are times when we need to receive "moisture" from the atmosphere around us. Jesus enclosed this world with an atmosphere of grace as real as the air we breathe. We need this grace every morning. "Now in the morning, having risen a long while before daylight, He [Jesus] went out and departed to a solitary place; and there He prayed" (Mark 1:35).

Jesus received divine power and wisdom while He prayed. Then, He went out to where the people were and shared what He had received.

As a follower of Christ, we daily seek Him, and then daily share what we have received. We are to give what the Holy Spirit has given us.

Christ's mission and method are the same for His followers. "As you sent Me into the world, I also have sent them into the world" (John 17:18).

 PRACTICAL PROJECT

As a family, get up early and check out your lawn. Can you find dew or guttation? Learn to tell the difference. Life is about receiving and giving, and learning how to keep a healthy balance.

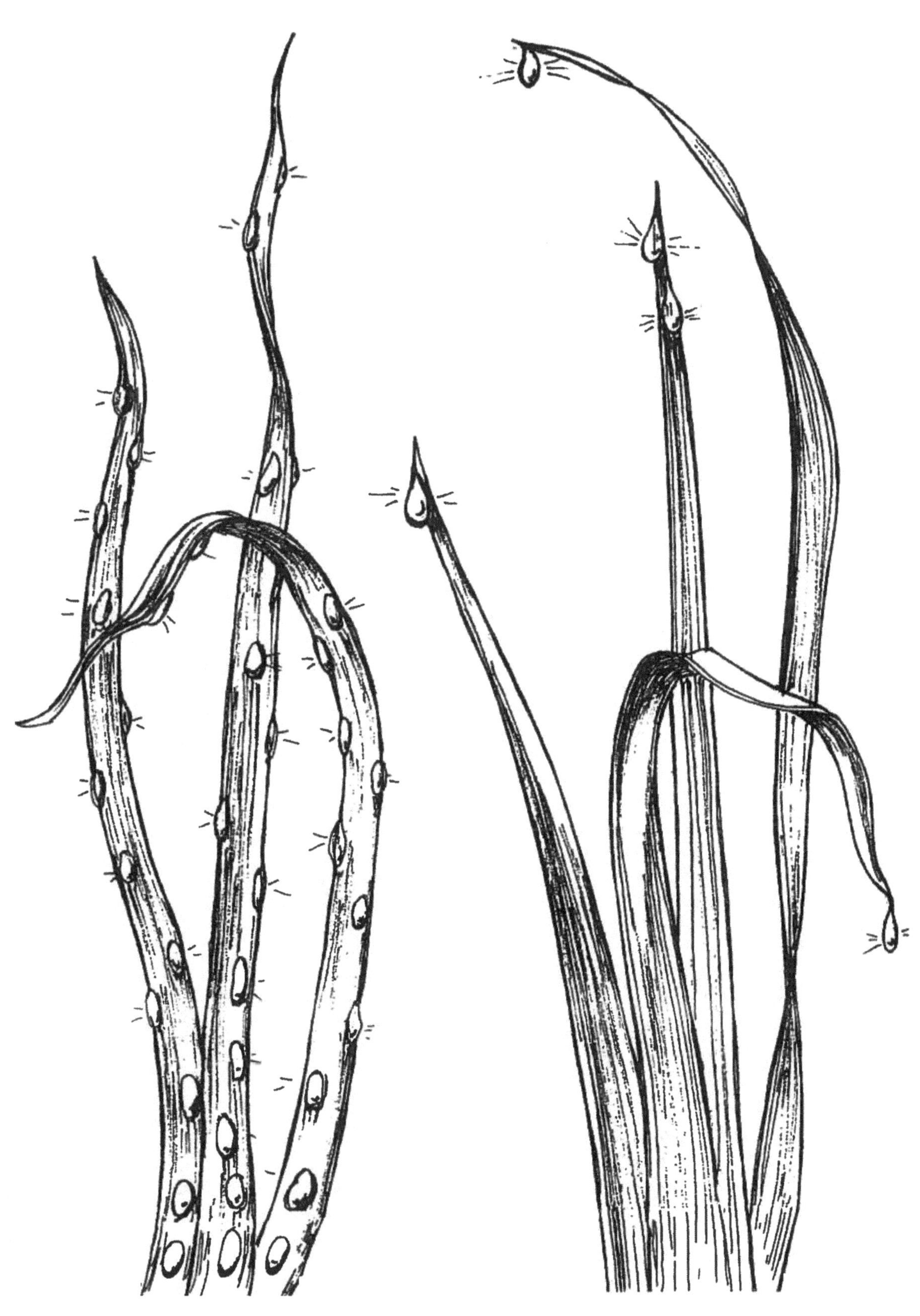

Five Common Grasses

The Gramineae family has unique characteristics that make them grass. From the flood until now, grass has spread its message of obedience to God's laws, and of His care for the lowly mission of grass. Today, one-fifth of the land surface of earth grows grass. With the growth of grass came the spread of animal and man. Below are listed some characteristics that describe grass. Christians, likewise, have certain characteristics that make them a follower of Christ. "You will know them by their fruits" (Matthew 7:16).

QUALITIES OF A CHRISTIAN	QUALITIES OF GRASS
1. A Christian is a follower of Jesus and lives His life. John 15:5	1. Grass has a round stem. It may be hollow like bamboo and field grass or pithy like corn and cereal grass.
2. Christians are one body joined together. Ephesians 4:15, 16	2. Grass is jointed with solid rings circling the joints.
3. Christians love one another. Ephesians 4:31, 32; Hebrews 10:24, 25	3. The leaf blade grows out of the rings. The ring's name is node.
4. Christians love and keep His commandments. John 14:15; 15:10; Revelation 12:17; 1 John 2:3–5	4. Leaves grow singly, one leaf per node, and alternately, on opposite sides of the stem. The lower part of the leaf is called the sheath and wraps around the stem. The upper part is called the blade. (See illustration, page 17)
5. Christian growth is from the inside out. Ephesians 3:16–21	5. Grass can survive much cutting because the blades grow from cells at the base of the sheath not from the tips. This type of growth is called intercellular growth.
6. Christians produce the fruits of the spirit. They seek to reproduce these fruits in others. John 15:5, 12, 16; Galatians 5:22–25; Romans 8:1, 4, 5	6. Grass is a flowering plant and produces seeds. Grass flowers are small, odorless, and almost colorless. They are wind or self-pollinated.
7. Christians live the cross of Christ. They depend not on circumstances, but on divinity. They grow where they are sent. Matthew 28:19, 20; 5:10–12	7. Grass can grow under hard conditions the world over. Ninety-eight percent of all agricultural land is grass.

PRACTICAL PROJECT

On the opposite page are five common grasses. By their characteristics, see if you can identify any of them growing near where you live. They are from left to right: 1. Orchard grass 2. Smooth meadow grass. 3. Timothy grass. 4. Wild oat grass. 5. Crested dogs tail grass.

Adaptability of Grass

God has made grass very adaptable. It grows over a wider range than any other family of flowering plants. It grows in deserts, swamps, and even on the tops of mountains.

Christians also must be adaptable to carry the gospel to the entire world. God's love is livable and adaptable to every climate, language, and culture of the world.

A blade of grass does not refuse to grow because it is not on a beautiful lawn. It can adapt and grow in the crack of a sidewalk. It will grow here without notice or appreciation.

Like grass, most of us work in our little niche without recognition or thanks. In this little place many are discontented. They feel their life is useless.

However, our little blade of grass growing in a crack will labor on, pouring out its bit of purified air. This little waft of air makes its way quietly through the city streets bearing its whiff of healthy vitality.

We need this lesson. Talent is too often praised and position sought. Some children will do nothing unless rewarded and praised. We need to learn faithful adaptability to the little jobs we are given.

As grass can adapt to a sidewalk's crack,
My little chore I will attack.
Man's praise I may not much attract,
God's favor, I surely will not lack.
"A faithful man will abound with blessings"
(Proverbs 28:20).

PRACTICAL PROJECT

Go for a walk around the block of your home. See how much grass grows in the cracks of your sidewalks. Try trading family chores and see how joyfully adaptable all can be.

Fire and Grass

It is estimated that some 1,800 thunderstorms are sweeping around the world at this moment. In the following 20 minutes lightning will strike some 60,000 times. In the spring before plants turn green and in the fall after vegetation dies, fire danger is the greatest. When a fire passes by, the soil remains blackened with ash and charred stubble. Fire burns off refuse and excess grass growing on the surface. Grass near the root level is less likely to be affected by fire.

Scripture uses grass to illustrate the wicked. Youth are tempted to envy the wicked because they do not see their end. God invites us to see the end of the wicked, even when they appear to be prospering.

After a fire an amazing rebirth takes place in nature; black soil absorbs more heat. As the heat increases, the grass seed, which is forever blowing in the wind, sprouts quickly.

"Do not fret because of evildoers, nor be envious of the workers of iniquity. For they shall soon be cut down like the grass, and whither as the green herb" (Psalm 37:1, 2).

Fire burns off the excess and makes room for new growth. In a similar way, God will do a cleansing work at the harvest of this earth. Read 2 Peter 3 to learn how God plans to remove sin from this world.

David said, "But the wicked shall perish; and the enemies of the Lord, like the splendor of the meadows, shall vanish. Into smoke they shall vanish away" (Psalm 37:20).

PRACTICAL PROJECT

Think what your house would be like if no one carried out the trash? What happens to the trash and the garbage after it leaves your home? Purpose to put into your life only that which is wholesome and safe for eternity.

Prairie and Grass

The world's largest grasslands used to be those of Europe and Asia. They once stretched unbroken from the meadows of the Danube Valley eastward nearly to the Pacific Ocean. Today, the former grasslands of North America have become the world's greatest source of wheat.

In the early 1850s, wheat farmers found that Iowa was covered with tall prairie grass. The soil beneath was composed of rich black humus often 12 feet deep. This was formed from the decomposition of countless grass roots back to the days of Noah after the flood. Five different types of grass grew on this prairie, some up to 12 feet tall. In the last one and one-half centuries man has decreased this humus to a mere few feet deep.

Today the vast grassland prairies have largely vanished.

With the disappearance of the prairies, the buffalo (North American Bison) almost vanished with them. Buffalo, by the millions, once freely roamed the grasslands. But man, by ignorance, greed, and indifference, nearly made them extinct. Like the prairies, our world is decaying away because of sin.

However, by careful conservation the buffalo have made a comeback and are thriving once again. This recovery of the buffalo gives us hope for the future.

Our earth, while blighted by the curse of sin is still rich in evidence, not only of creation, but also of re-creation. In the springtime we see God's restorative power at work when the prairies turn green again. "For I will pour water on him, who is thirsty, and floods on the dry ground; I will pour My Spirit on your descendants, and My blessing on your offspring; they will spring up among the grass like willows by the watercourses" (Isaiah 44:3, 4).

Tender spires of grass spring out of the ground and reveal God's recovery power. "And He shall be like the light of the morning when the sun rises, a morning without clouds, like the tender grass springing out of the earth, by clear shining after rain" (2 Samuel 23:4).

The prairie in spring becomes to us a symbol of living hope. While the vast prairies have largely vanished, their remnant spires of springing green tell of the divine power to restore. "Nevertheless we, according to His promise, look for a new heaven and a new earth in which righteousness dwells" (2 Peter 3:13).

From creation until now, the common blade of grass still declares, "God is love."

PRACTICAL PROJECT

Plan to visit one of the National Grassland parks in North or South Dakota; Wyoming; New Mexico; or Saskatchewan, Canada. Plan to camp out and enjoy the space, the sky, the wind, the silence, the grass, and each other in God's great out-of-door classroom. Take this book along and enjoy the time and space. What will heaven be like?

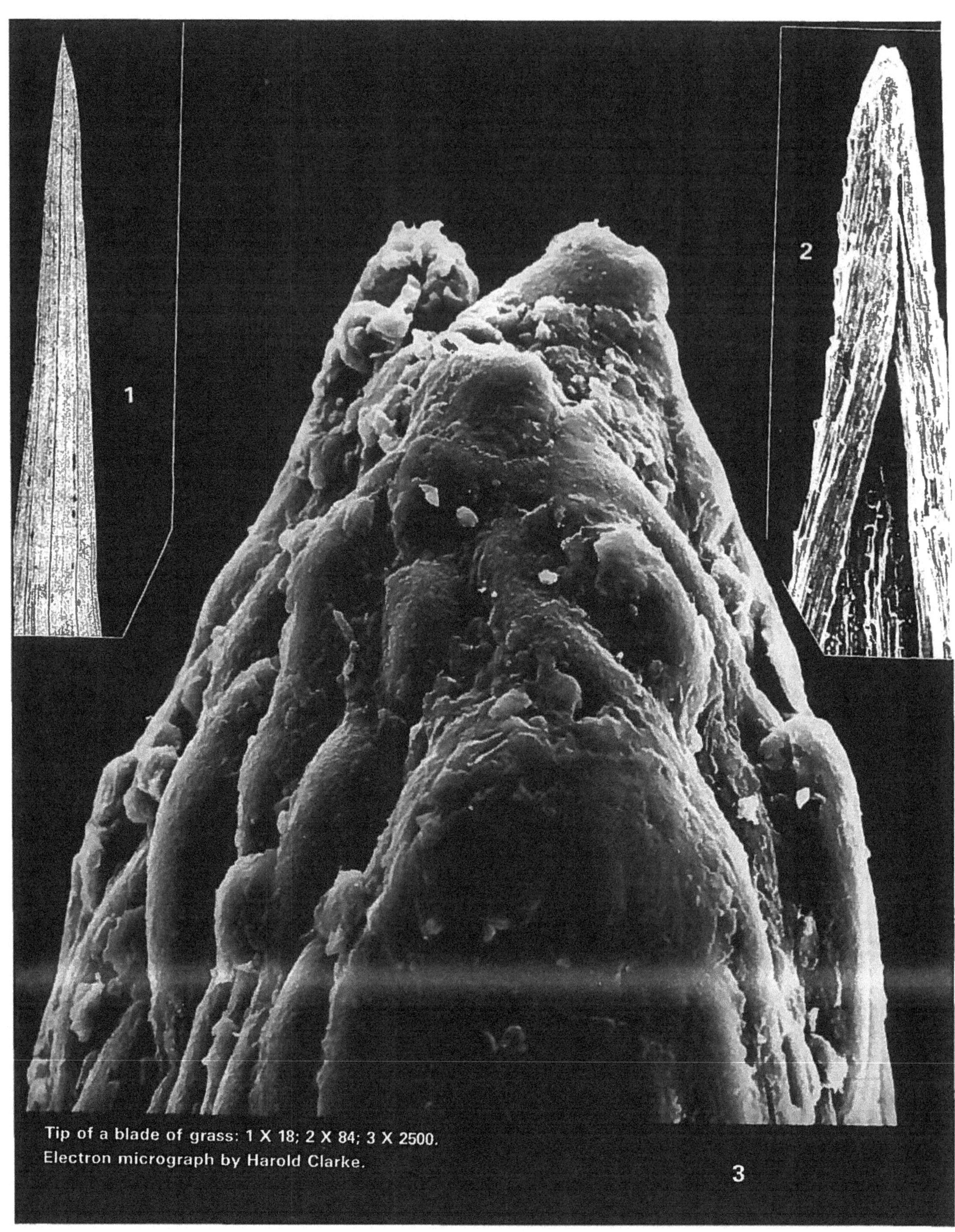

Tip of a blade of grass at three different magnifications.

The Gospel According to Creation Seminars

Terry McComb, Speaker and Writer with *Creation Illustrated* magazine, has conducted countless character-building, Bible-based seminars that reveal eternal truths through the handiwork of God. The Spiritual messages have a lasting impact on all ages and include black-light chalk drawings with his wife's soft piano artistry in the background.

Pastor McComb has authored more than 50 articles with *Creation Illustrated* magazine and co-authored with his wife Jean, five children's books for parents to study with their children—*Gospel According to a Dandelion; Gospel According to a Blade of Grass; Gospel According to a Snowflake; Gospel According to a Thornless Blackberry;* and *Gospel According to a Tree.*

Available Seminars (available for purchase as a digital download or DVD copy):

"The Creation Story" is a scientific walk through Genesis one. How does each day of the Creation Week reveal its Author and how is this truth relevant to our spiritual walk? A nine-hour seminar from Sunday through Saturday night.

"In His Image" focuses on the wonder of the human body! This nine-hour seminar is a fast-moving study that examines the 12 systems of the body and their amazing designer. Deeply scientific, yet spiritual.

"The Wonder of a Tree" is a nine-hour seminar illustrating how the lifestyle, function, and ways of a tree reveal the ways of its Creator, Jesus Christ.

"Creations Creator" is a five-hour week-end seminar that addresses evolution vs. creation and the truth about Dinosaurs. Topics include: The Cross as Seen in Nature, Worship Him Who Made, Heart Reading Nature, and the Gospel According to a Dandelion power point presentation with music background.

"How to Heart Read Nature" will help viewers learn how to see past the trees and see the Creator. This is a hands-on practical nine-hour seminar that uses the out-of-doors classroom and needs to be in a nature setting. Short on theory and long on active learning.

"The Heavens are Telling" deals with The Gospel According to Astronomy" with plenty of NASA space telescope photos. This nine-hour seminar shows God's ways in outer space to help fill your heart's inner space with His love.

These Seminars can be done by Zoom
To Book a Seminar or order books and DVD's
Call: (250) 547-6696
E-mail: terry@gospelcreation.com
Web site: www.gospelcreation.com
Write: The Gospel According to Creation Seminar
39 Pine Road, Cherryville, British Columbia, Canada V0E 2G3

www.ingramcontent.com/pod-product-compliance
Lightning Source LLC
LaVergne TN
LVHW060642110826
845147LV00018B/1026

* 9 7 8 1 4 7 9 6 1 2 4 0 6 *